LATOYA MICHELLE HOPWOOD'S

GOD IS *REALLY* NICE

21 DAYS TO TALK ABOUT 21 TRAITS GOD HAS BUT NO ONE TALKS ABOUT

This book is dedicated to my beautiful grandmother, Josephine Hopwood. I picked up your fruit Grandma.

God Is Really Nice.
Copyright 2025 by Latoya Michelle Hopwood.
All rights reserved. Printed in the United States of America. No part of this book may be used or reproduced in any manner whatsoever without written permission except in the case of brief quotations embodied in articles and reviews.
Graphics and photos from Canva.com
Summary: Knowing more about God.
– Provided by author.
ISBN: 979-8-9923366-0-3 (Paperback)
1. Christian Life prayer 2.Inspiration and Personal Growth/Development

introduction
Hello!

Think about it, I mean really think about it, God is the absolute best. There is no one better than Him, but we don't hear a lot of this. Many people teach us that we better run to God because there is a devil loose, but does anyone take the time to really dive into other reasons we should want to be around Him? We all know He will avenge us and He's omnipresent and full of grace, but did you also know He is the God of soft skills? He's more than a Father, Protector, and Provider, God is so beautiful. Just take that in. I know you haven't heard how beautiful He is, but He is. He is breathtakingly amazing from the inside out. I love the Bible, but there are purposely no verses in this book. I want you to experience how God will fill in the blanks and whatever you need, God, Jesus, and/or The Holy Spirit will tell you.

Suggestion: As you learn more about God, do yourself a favor and also take the next 21 days to pray and fast ***into*** something you've been meaning to do. Fasting is not about taking away, it's about ***inviting in***. I**nv**ite God to have meals with you. **Invite** The Holy Spirit to watch movies with you. **Invite** Jesus to help you make a new friend or goal list. I'm told it takes our brains 21 days to create a habit, so, if there is something you've been meaning to ***grow in***, take the next 21 days to fast into it. As you invite more of God in, He'll replace that old want with new ideas from Him.

- let's - pray

Heavenly Father, thank you for opening my eyes to see you in other ways. For the next 21 days, guide my thoughts and steps. I know who you are to me now and I am so excited to learn more. Our time together will be blessed. In the name of Jesus, I pray, Amen.

really nice; like fragrantly kind.

Mannnnn...if you only knew how sweet God is. Have you ever eaten something so delicious that you had to pause just to acknowledge how someone may have put their foot in it? That's how sweet God is. God is so nice, He smells good. His sweetness actually surprises people. Merriam-Webster defines nice as 'stresses great precision and delicacy of adjustment or discrimination'. God is beautifully delicate in how He loves us and He wants us to be delicate with Him, others, and ourselves too. Be really nice, like fragrantly kind, just like our God. God is really nice.

happy.

Ever seen someone after they've made a change? After they finally did what they'd been dreaming of? They look so happy. They look happy because the smile they are wearing is genuine; it's coming from the inside. This is how God is. He is genuinely happy. Happiness follows Him because He is happiness. That does not mean He doesn't get disappointed or sad but it does mean He doesn't stay there. So the next time you think of God, think of a God who is smiling and laughing, and a God who is full of joy because that's who He is. God is really happy.

gentle.

God is the kind of gentle that you see when you're on a beach and the waves are calmingly rolling in. Not only does God have the gentlest touch, but He handles situations with the utmost care. God is constantly considering your feelings and at the same time, He ensures your anger, your hopelessness, your bitterness, and your need for revenge, all disappear. Think of His touch and His awareness towards your situation the way the softest material feels against your body. That is how gentle our God is. When you go about your day, take a moment to think about Our Father's gentleness. God is really gentle.

caring.

When I say God will go out of His way to find you, to get you, to make sure you are okay, I mean it. I know some people think, do I really want God as a father if He would sacrifice His only Son for me? But God knew Jesus would be better than okay. He knew He would be able to take care of His Son and because of His Son's sacrifice, take care of us too. He cared enough for us as children, siblings, and co-heirs of Christ to allow His only begotten Son to sacrifice himself for us. If that isn't care, what is? I promise you, God is a Father who cares about the littlest things from the type of coffee you're having that morning to big things like who you plan on getting in business with. God is really caring.

great listener.

God is the most amazing listener. He can hear what we're saying and what we're not saying. God can listen to present complaints while hearing our future dreams. When we stand in front of God, we stand complete, so all of the complaining and carrying on is considered, but not impressionable. God knows how we really feel and when we complain, although it will not take us out, He still listens with a gracious heart and open ear because we think it will. Then, just so we know He was listening and because He cares so much for us, He fixes whatever concerns we have. As a bonus, because God can also hear what we don't say, God fixes that too. God is a really great listener.

doer.

God gets things done. He is a God of action. When you tell Him things like someone hurt you, or when there are things in your life that need to get done, God is on it. God was on it before you thought you needed Him to be on it. He ensures angels are out and doing what they need to do. God also ensures we have what we need. He changes His plans to make sure that we can get done what He puts in our hearts to do. He is the brilliant creator of universes, of people, of dreams. God is not lazy, and yet He knows when to rest. God is never sitting on the sidelines, He's in the game, and He's making sure that He's doing whatever He can so you and your loved ones will win. God really is a doer.

rooting for you.

This characteristic of God changed my life. Did you know God is rooting for you? He wants you to succeed. He wants you to find love. He wants your business ideas to work out. He truly wants you to be happy. The Holy Spirit told me this and I couldn't believe it. Some of us believe God forsakes us during tough times and He is making life harder so He can teach us a lesson, but God is actually hoping for our best. God is our biggest cheerleader. He wants us to pull through and it brings Him so much joy when we realize He is rooting for us. We have the God of all gods on our side. Push your shoulders back, remember who belong to, and hold your head up high. God is really rooting for you.

creative.

Who do you know more creative than God? And I'm not talking about complex things like molecules, planets floating by themselves in space, multiple galaxies, mitosis, and/or the magic of stem cells, I'm talking about who do you know that decides after it rains, I'm going to put a rainbow in the sky? Who thinks I'm going to make two insects, butterflies and dragonflies and I'm going to make them different from each other? Who with their ingenuity and power decides to separate water from the sky or create beautiful floating land and calls them islands? I don't know anyone who can imagine the sheer complexities and beauty of an ocean reef. This world is full of His exceptional wonders due to His unmatched creativity. God is really creative.

positive.

God is extremely positive. When you come to Him with all your woes, doubts, and other things weighing you down, He's so positive He doesn't even have the space around Him for it. He calmly says, "Just give it to me. I got it. Everything will be okay, and not only when you give it to me, am I going to absolutely put it in the place where it's forgotten, I won't dig it up to remember it." That's incomparable positivity. God is so positive, He radiates. God is so full of positivity, He literally shines. He is hope. He is actual hope. So God, who is actual hope, can't be negative. Now, does this mean He's happy all the time, absolutely not, but what you're not going to do is go to God, and He'll tell you something that is the opposite of the light He is. God is really positive and really full of joy.

truthful.

God's truth is the only truth that matters. When God says something, believe it. God can't lie because He desires not to lie. So when God says that you are righteous because He made you that way, He's telling the truth, believe Him. When God says He will never leave you, He's telling the truth, believe Him. When God says He loves you, believe Him. God's truth is finitely honest and always working. Sometimes we don't want to hear the truth and God knows it. So with supernatural care and grace, God tells us what we need to hear, freeing us from what we don't want to hear. God's truth is a testament to His unwavering love and the cornerstone of our faith. God is really truthful.

peaceful.

Did you know we serve a God who avoids arguments? Because of His peace, chaos is nowhere to be found, therefore there are no arguments. God doesn't like to argue. He is not the screaming, petty, or vindictive type. The kind of peace that surrounds God is indescribable. There's a stillness in His presence that takes away any and every cruel thing. He will wait patiently while you make horrible decisions and still be there with arms wide open, ready to help you experience His peace. When you experience His peace, it's as if everything around you is in slow motion. Everything is calm. Everything is beautiful. Everything is God.

God really is peaceful.

love.

Because of His love, He will always be in your corner. God's love fights for you even when you have no idea you're in a fight. God's love can't fail. The love God has for you renews every morning and tucks you in every night. His love is like the fluffiest of clouds and the perfect beam of sunlight. God's love follows you to work and school. It announces your arrival and prepares your return. His love goes into your future just to see what will make you smile and then brings it back to you in memory, deja vu, coincidences, flashbacks, or smiles. God's love promises things only He can fulfill. His love carves paths only His love can make. God's love is so vast, it reaches trillions and trillions of things at once. Every cell, every raindrop, every tick of your clock has God's love in it. God really is love.

funny.

God is very, very, funny! I know you didn't think all of these funny people just pulled this characteristic out of the air. Laughter is not only a great thing, it's a God thing. God loves laughing so much, He designed laughter to bring us together and reduce stress. Some people may think God is never laughing at you and only with you but that's not true. God finds a lot of things we do funny. We bring God joy. He chuckles here and there all the time, especially when we say something funny or get tripped up. Our goofiness makes us laugh at ourselves and He laughs too. I can only imagine how God sounds when He is really cracking up. God also really enjoys how clever we are and He clearly has a sense of humor. Do you see some of the animals? Look at them, really take a good look at them. Some of them have to be for pure enjoyment. God is really funny.

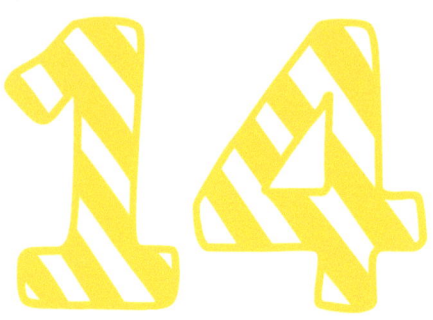

likes surprises.

God really likes surprises but in a good way. God will give a situation you're in an unimaginable, unexpected, more than you ever dreamed of end. God is not doing this to hurt anyone, He just knows what you desire. We get very distracted to the point where we don't know what makes us happy so it's a blessing to have a Father who knows what brings us authentic joy, even if it is a surprise. Most of us could never imagine our destiny being what it is and it's even more mind-blowing the new directions and heights we take. We have to blink more than twice when we realize we are living what we prayed for. God loves our surprised reactions. To God, it's not that we don't have faith, it's more so we are shocked by His exceedingly abundantly above all we can ask or think gifts. Our tears of joy are not unbelief, they are raw happiness. Only God knows what makes us truly happy and if He chooses to blow our minds through personalized surprises, then let Him. God really likes surprises.

relentless.

God is really relentless. God keeps showing up and He's not letting you go. He's not giving up on you and He will always be there for you, no matter what. God will go after you and your loved ones with everything He has. God cares so much that even when you say no, He says yes. There are plenty of people in the Bible who told God that they couldn't do something, and God was relentless in convincing them they could. Moses thought there was no way he could free God's people but God relentlessly conquered Moses' fears and doubts. Sarah thought there was no way she and Abraham were having a son but God made sure His promise came true. Our Father has the same tenacity when it comes to us. He created relentless tenacity just for us. He will get us to see the vision and with a spirit of divine relentlessness give us the tools to live out His supernatural dreams i.e. the desires of His heart. God is really relentless.

defender.

God is a defender, not only physically, and emotionally but God defends reputations and dreams too. God loves us so much He will send The Holy Spirit on assignment into dreams, emails, DM's, ads, posts on social media, interrupt conversations, and soften people's hearts just to defend you. And sometimes God is not bringing you to these people's attention just so they know who you are, He does this to push back against loneliness, poverty, misalignment, or any other kind of lack in your life. He whispers in your future and helps your destiny fight against any distractions. He puts walls between you, self-doubt, and unbearable hardships. In business, He blocks your enemies from spreading lies about you. In your personal life, He defends the reputation of your partner for His name's sake and the prosperity of your blessed bloodline. Our Father goes toe to toe when it comes to you, He has never lost a battle, and He never will. God is really the greatest defender.

smart.

There are no words to describe how intelligent God is. The way God plans and executes the smallest of things is unbelievably remarkable. Who creates oxygen and tells it what to do? Who creates oceans and tells them where to roll? Who creates the wind and tells it where it can blow? Who decides the only way to save us is to make us like Jesus, Our Savior? God created the moon and stars and gave them each a purpose. God tells plants they will be green, flowers they will be yellow, and Bluebirds they will be blue. God desires it and it purposely and beautifully happens. God created us with the power to do the same. We too can desire and only with the graceful help of God, make it happen. Everything God does is so purposefully perfect and remarkably smart. God is really smart.

fighter.

God is a fighter. When one way doesn't work, God finds another way. God never gives up on mankind. He put a bow in the sky, sent His Son to die, raised Him to sit on the throne, and gifted us with His Holy Spirit as proof. God has a fight for us that no other god has. Our Father makes ways when there is no possible way. He builds bridges where there are no connections, places calmness in the middle of chaotic storms, and sets the greenest of oases amid the driest of deserts. Our Father steps into the ring when we had no idea there was a fight. He stands in the face of our trembling enemies, dares them to touch us, and sets a covering over us like no other. He fights our lack of identity every day, reminding us of who we are and who we belong to. In the mighty and miraculous name of Jesus, Our Father is really an amazing, mind-blowing, undefeated fighter.

aesthetics.

God is all about aesthetics. Who am I kidding, God is the epitome of aesthetics. God smells good, looks good, and loves beautiful things. God paints this world beautifully by just using His words. Breathtaking landscapes exist all over the world because of Our Father. Beautiful sunrises, sunsets, islands made from fire, full moon walks on secluded beaches, and coral reefs filled with all types of beautifully made things are all because of Our Father. God is really beautiful. Aesthetically He is pure awe and sheer greatness. God looks and feels familiar, kind, and powerful. God's fragrance completely engulfs wherever He is and He leaves a residue of captivating glory wherever He goes. God is really into aesthetics.

patient.

God really is patient. Despite all the screaming, accusations, and wrongful persecutions, God waits for you to realize who He is to you, a patient and caring Father. God is a Father who is here to love you, protect you, provide for you, and patiently help you. God's patience is so pure and good, He makes it sharable, pouring it into us so we too can experience the strength of knowing no matter what, God will make this happen. God's patience has no limitations and doesn't check a clock. When you are His child, it is something He freely and willingly gifts to you. God will be off in a corner waiting for you to realize He was there the entire time, wanting to help you have a life beyond your wildest dreams. God's patience is divine. It reaches into areas of your life where nothing else can go. God's patience is calming and devoted to carrying you throw storms. His patience has a best friend called Faith. These two together help God's children to see how God himself equipped us to be supernaturally unstoppable.

God is really patient.

cries.

God cries. You can really hurt God's feelings but you can also make Him cry tears of joy. When God cries tears of joy, the Earth celebrates too. Waves roll smooth, trees sway, and flowers bloom as they all enjoy God's happy tears. Your triumphs make God cry. It doesn't matter if you think they are big or small, God is still so proud of you. God knows your heart, so when you go through anything hurtful and come out better than good, God is happy for you. God cries when you get it, when you understand Him more, and especially when you are happy. God absolutely lives off making His children smile. He loves to see us happy and enjoying life. God cries when we cry. Sometimes we just fall apart but in the best way. When we think of how good God is, we begin to weep uncontrollable tears of joy. A wave of gratefulness pours out of us like nobody's business and when this happens, God cries too. He knows how grateful you are and how your heart is full of love. He knows that you know, you love Him, and believe that with Him, anything is possible. God really cries.

100 More Things About Our God

1. God is not a settler.
2. God is full of grace.
3. God is powerful.
4. God is diligent.
5. God is beautiful.
6. God is the maker of beautiful things.
7. God is The Creator.
8. God is The Giver.
9. God is a receiver.
10. God is a loving Father.
11. God is a caretaker.
12. God is a believer in you.
13. God is The Truth.
14. God is life.
15. God is The Healer.
16. God is The Waymaker.
17. God is The Undefeated.
18. God is precious.
19. God is a delight.
20. God is a wonder.
21. God is a safe haven.
22. God is a strong tower.
23. God is The Hero.
24. God is The Financial Blessing.
25. God is The Emotional Blessing.
26. God is The Comforter.
27. God is a plan maker.
28. God is the lover of our souls.
29. God is forward-thinking.
30. God is all-knowing.
31. God is innovative.
32. God is respectful.
33. God is a secure guider.
34. God is unique.
35. God is The Aligner.
36. God is the right kind of support.
37. God is intentionally purposeful.
38. God is a God of discretion.
39. God is empathetic.
40. God is a safe space.
41. God is harmonious.
42. God is accountable.
43. God is an open book.
44. God is The DreamMaker.
45. God is The Dream Executor.
46. God is the table setter.
47. God is the revenge seeker.
48. God is forgiveness.
49. God is a soft place to land.
50. God is The One you need to turn to.
51. God is a divine helper.
52. God is the King of Kings.
53. God is the connector and corrector.
54. God is a refiner.
55. God is a gentle reminder.
56. God is a seeker of His children.
57. God is The Builder.
58. God is a refreshing presence.
59. God is the best shoulder to cry on.
60. God is never wrong.

100 More Things About Our God con't

61. God is not an abuser.
62. God is always watching.
63. God is The Light.
64. God is the air we breathe.
65. God is the core of our existence.
66. God is the head of our households.
67. God is the CEO of our companies.
68. God is the decision maker.
69. God is pure.
70. God is humble.
71. God is the grower of dreams.
72. God is a promise keeper.
73. God is the doctor in the sick room and the lawyer in the courtroom.
74. God is considerate.
75. God is the touchdown, the 3-point shot, the homerun... the winning play.
76. God is the goal.
77. God is beyond witty.
78. God is always available to you.
79. God is not messing around when it comes to you.
80. God is a fixer.
81. God is a warm hug when you need Him.
82. God is the glow everyone sees in you.
83. God is hope.
84. God is faith.
85. God is the lifeline in the knick of time.
86. God is a lifeguard in the sea of sorrow.
87. God is joy and hope for tomorrow.
88. God is a friend.
89. God is a praiser.
90. God is everywhere.
91. God is never leaving you or forsaking you.
92. God is surrounding you.
93. God is The First and The Last.
94. God is The Only Way.
95. God is The True and Living God.
96. God is anything you need Him to be.
97. God is limitless and unbounding.
98. God is divine rest assured.
99. God is over-the-top and mind-blowing.
100. God is our God.

www.ingramcontent.com/pod-product-compliance
Lightning Source LLC
LaVergne TN
LVHW010027070426
835510LV00001B/14